HIP-HOP DANCING

BREAKING

VOLUME 2

by Wendy Garofoli

Consultant:
AleKsa "LeX" Chmiel, Co-Director/Owner
Flomotion Dance Company
Philadelphia, Pennsylvania

CAPSTONE PRESS
a capstone imprint

Velocity is published by Capstone Press,
151 Good Counsel Drive, P.O. Box 669, Mankato, Minnesota 56002.
www.capstonepub.com

Books published by Capstone Press are manufactured with paper
containing at least 10 percent post-consumer waste.

Library of Congress Cataloging-in-Publication Data
Garofoli, Wendy.
Hip-hop dancing / by Wendy Garofoli.
p. cm.
Includes bibliographical references and index.
Summary: "Provides step-by-step instructions for learning breaking, popping, locking,
and krumping hip-hop dance moves"—Provided by publisher.
ISBN 978-1-4296-5484-5 (library binding)—ISBN 978-1-4296-5485-2 (library
binding)—ISBN 978-1-4296-5486-9 (library binding)—ISBN 978-1-4296-5487-6
(library binding)
1. Hip-hop dance. I. Title.
GV1796.H57G37 2011
793.3—dc22   2010030394

Editorial Credits
Megan Peterson and Jennifer Besel, editors; Veronica Correia, designer; Marcie Spence,
    media researcher; Sarah Schuette, photo stylist; Laura Manthe, production specialist

Photo Credits
Capstone Studio: Karon Dubke, 24, 25, 26 (bottom), 30, 31, 36 (top), 37, 38, 39, TJ
Thoraldson Digital Photography, cover, 5, 6, 7, 8, 10, 11, 12, 13, 14, 15, 16, 17, 18, 19,
20, 21, 22, 23, 26 (top), 27, 28, 29, 32, 33, 34, 35, 36 (bottom), 40, 41, 42, 43, 44, 45;
Shutterstock: Andreas Gradin, 4

Printed in the United States of America in Stevens Point, Wisconsin.
092010   005934WZS11

TABLE OF CONTENTS

THESE ARE THE BREAKS

It's a cool evening in the Bronx, New York, in the 1970s. A DJ plays a record at a block party. As the music blasts, a crowd forms a circle. One by one, dancers come to the middle of the circle to show off their moves. They're dancing in a funky new style called breaking. They don't know it now, but the style will grow to become a worldwide craze.

Today breaking is more popular than ever. The style has changed from a party dance to an important dance form. Breakers, also called b-boys and b-girls, learn moves in several different categories.

DROPS:
moves that bring breakers down to the floor

TOPROCK AND UPROCK:
breaking moves performed while standing up

POWER MOVES:
advanced moves like the Windmill and Head Spin

FLOOR WORK:
moves performed on the ground

FREEZES:
stylish poses that usually involve balancing

TONE UP

STRENGTHENING EXERCISES

In order to pull off any breaking move, dancers need both style and strength. You must have strong arm, back, and stomach muscles. You must also stretch your muscles before attempting any of the moves in this book. Here are a few exercises to get you started.

ARMS AND CHEST: Do a set of push-ups. Tighten your stomach muscles, and keep your body straight while you do your push-ups.

STOMACH: Do as many sit-ups or crunches as you can. Work different muscles by twisting to the right or left as you crunch your stomach muscles.

BICEPS: Hold a 5-pound (2.3-kilogram) dumbbell or large can of soup in your right hand. Keep your right arm straight by your side. Slowly bend your elbow, and lift the weight toward your chest. Then lower the weight. Continue doing biceps curls until you start to feel your muscles burn. Repeat with the left arm.

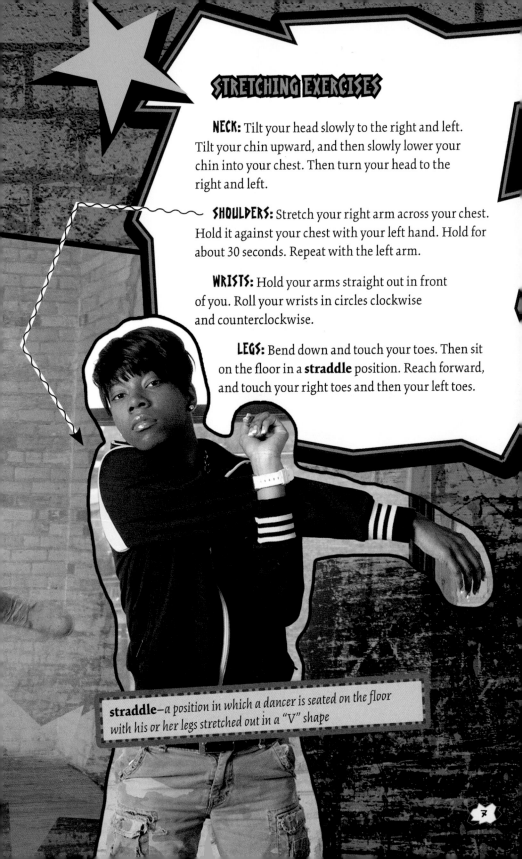

STRETCHING EXERCISES

NECK: Tilt your head slowly to the right and left. Tilt your chin upward, and then slowly lower your chin into your chest. Then turn your head to the right and left.

SHOULDERS: Stretch your right arm across your chest. Hold it against your chest with your left hand. Hold for about 30 seconds. Repeat with the left arm.

WRISTS: Hold your arms straight out in front of you. Roll your wrists in circles clockwise and counterclockwise.

LEGS: Bend down and touch your toes. Then sit on the floor in a **straddle** position. Reach forward, and touch your right toes and then your left toes.

straddle—*a position in which a dancer is seated on the floor with his or her legs stretched out in a "V" shape*

GEAR

It might seem like b-boys and b-girls dance in their street clothes. But many choose specific gear in order to perform at their best.

Helmets or skullcaps help protect your head during floor work and freezes.

Wristbands pad your wrists and elbows during floor work and freezes.

Knee pads protect your knees during drops and floor work.

Loose-fitting pants and shirts allow for ease of movement.

Sneakers with good traction help you grip the floor.

Don't wear a shirt that's too baggy. While balancing upside down in difficult freezes, it could slip down and block your view.

Left and Right

As you learn breaking moves, remember to practice them to the left and to the right. The step-by-step instructions in this book only tell you how to complete a move to one side. But you will eventually need to master both sides, especially if you plan on competing in a **battle** someday. Sometimes dancers will win battles simply by showing they can perform breaking moves to the left and to the right.

Start by learning the move on the side that feels most comfortable for you. Once you get the hang of the move on that side, reverse the steps. It may feel awkward at first, but eventually you'll get the hang of it. Being able to perform the move both ways makes you a better all-around dancer.

Breaking Influences

Breaking got its start in the Bronx in the 1970s. But the style is influenced by other forms of movement created in the United States and around the world. These influences include:

- an Afro-Brazilian dance style called **capoeira** (kah-puh-WAY-ruh)
- Kung-Fu moves in 1970s movies
- swing dancing
- Latin dance styles such as the salsa

battle—*a competition between individual dancers or groups*
capoeira—*a Brazilian dance of African origin that uses martial arts moves such as kicks and chops*

Chapter 1

TOPROCK AND UPROCK

Side-To-Side

DIFFICULTY: ★

The **Side-to-Side** is a simple toprock step. Breakers use this move to help them find the music's **rhythm**. Dancers often perform it while they're waiting in the **cypher**.

Step 1

Stand in a relaxed position with both feet together. Step out to the right with your right foot. Most of your weight remains on your left foot.

rhythm—a regular beat in music or dance
cypher—a circle that forms around a breaker to give space to dance during a battle

Step 2

Step together. Shift your weight to your right foot. Pick up your left foot, and step out to the left. Step together. Repeat the Side-to-Side for as long as you'd like.

You can use any arm movement during the Side-to-Side. A classic arm movement is to slightly bend your arms at the elbows, and hold them straight in front of you. Your hands should be in fists. Each time you step, roll your arms up and away from your body.

Kick Step
DIFFICULTY: ★★☆

The **Kick Step** is a toprock move that looks just how it sounds. You'll kick and step out to the side, all with a little bit of bounce.

Step ①

Stand with your feet together. Kick your right foot forward, keeping it fairly low to the ground.

Step 2

Step down with your right foot in front of your left foot.

Step 3

Step out to the left and slightly behind you with your left foot. Keeping your legs where they are, pick up your right foot, then set it down. Now repeat the Kick Step to the left, this time starting by kicking with your left foot.

TIP

The Kick Step is meant to be bouncy. After you get the hang of where your feet go, add a small hop to each step.

Add a little twist to your toprock moves with the **Crossover**. The more attitude you bring to the steps, the better the move will look!

Crossover

DIFFICULTY ★★★

Step 1

Stand with your feet together. Kick your right foot forward.

Step 2

Step back to the starting position with your right foot. Then kick your left foot forward.

Step 3

Step in front of your right foot with your left foot. At the same time, twist your body so that you face slightly to the left. Kick your right foot up behind you.

Step 4

not shown

Step back onto your right foot so that you face forward again. To repeat the Crossover, kick your left foot forward. Then step in front of your left foot with your right foot.

TiP

You can double up on the Crossover by repeating Step 3 before returning to face front.

Uprock Combination

DIFFICULTY: ⭐☆

Uprock is a type of rhythmic breaking move that's used for battling. It involves a swift jerk of the body and a drop to a squatting position. End the move by **burning** your opponent with an arm movement.

Step **1**

Stand in a relaxed position. Step forward with your right foot. Quickly kick your left foot behind you. As you step forward with the right foot, throw both arms forward then back.

burn—*to mimic or make fun of another dancer during an uprock move*

Step 2

Jump back on your left foot and kick your right foot forward. At the same time, throw your arms forward and hunch your shoulders.

Step 3

Now step your right foot next to your left foot, and push your hips forward. At the same time, drop your arms to your sides. Drop down into a squat position. Put your hands on your knees.

Step 4 *not shown*

Pop back up to a standing position. Burn your opponent with any type of arm movement. Pretend to hit a baseball out of the park or blow a kiss.

Tip

When you drop to a squat in Step 3, don't let your weight fall back on your heels. Keep your weight on your toes so you can easily stand back up.

Chapter 2

DROPS

Corkscrew

DIFFICULTY: ★★

In order to get to the floor, breakers need drops. A **Corkscrew** is a drop done with one foot hooked behind the opposite knee. This spinning drop will bring you down to the ground in style.

Step 1

Stand with your feet shoulder-width apart. Jump to the right with your left foot. Kick your right foot out to the side.

Step 2

Hook your right foot behind your left knee. Make sure your right toes are on the outside of your left knee.

Step 3

Fall down to the left. Land first on your right toes, and then catch the rest of your weight with your hands. Lean forward slightly so you don't fall backward or to the side. You should land with your legs crossed.

Step 4

Push up with your hands. Twirl your body to the right, uncrossing your legs as you stand up.

Tip

Make sure you don't let your knees touch the ground when you drop. Your right toes and your hands should hold all of your weight.

Sweep Drop

DIFFICULTY: 2

The **Sweep Drop** is a **transition** step. Breakers use it to move from toprocking into the Six-Step.

Step 1

Stand in a relaxed position with your feet together. Take a big step forward with your right foot. Lower your body to the floor, leaning slightly forward and bending your right knee. Touch your left hand to the floor for support.

transition—a step performed in order to move from one dance step to another

As you sweep your left leg around, pretend your left foot is the tip of a compass. Draw an imaginary half circle from the back of your body to the front using your foot.

Step 2

As you get closer to the floor, begin to sweep your left foot forward. Your left foot should pass between your right foot and left hand. You should land in a squat on your right foot with your left leg held straight in front of you.

B-Boy and B-Girl Names

Many b-boys and b-girls perform under stage names. Some dancers invent their own names. Others are given names by their fellow dancers. New York breaker Ephrat Asherie dances under the name B-Girl Bounce. Her fellow dancers gave her the nickname when they noticed her style was very bouncy and light. If you want a b-boy or b-girl name, here are a few things to consider:

• What's your style of breaking? Are you bold, smooth, or laid-back?

• Do you have a favorite move? Are your toprock moves better than your drops?

• Where do you live? Can you include your hometown or street name in your nickname?

If you can't come up with a name right away, don't worry. Your fellow dancers will help you out!

FLOOR WORK

Kickout

DIFFICULTY: ☆

One of the easiest floor work moves breakers perform is the **Kickout**. With one hand on the ground, a dancer kicks her heels forward. Then she pulls her feet back underneath her.

Step 1

Sit in a squat position. Place your right hand on the ground behind you, close to your right hip. Your left hand should be held against your body. Both feet are planted on the ground in front of you. Your backside should be slightly off the floor.

Step 2

Kick both feet wide out in front of you, keeping your feet on the floor. At the same time, extend your left arm in the air. Then scoot your legs back up to the starting position.

TIP

When you extend your legs in Step 2, your body should be in a straight line from your chest to your feet. Be sure to keep your backside lifted. If you let your hips drop, it is much more

The **Four-Step** is a **variation** on the famous Six-Step floor work move. It eliminates two of the steps but still keeps you rotating around on the floor.

Four-Step

DIFFICULTY: ★★

Step 1

Sit in a squat position. Place both hands on the floor behind you. Extend your right leg straight out in front of you.

Step 2

Switch your legs. Scoot your right leg back underneath you, and extend your left leg straight out in front of you. Your hands are still on the floor.

variation—something that is slightly different from another thing of the same type

Step  3

Lift your right arm and lean over to the left. Place your right hand on the floor next to your left hand. At the same time, bend your left knee and cross your left leg in front of your right leg.

Step 4

Shoot both legs straight behind you. You should land in a push-up position.

Step 5 *not shown*

Hop back to the position in Step 1. You should be squatting on your left foot with your right leg extended in front of you.

Repeat the Four-Step four times to make a complete circle and face front once again.

Baby Swipe

The **Baby Swipe** is a fast-paced floor work move that's anything but babyish. It requires a lot of torso twisting, leg sweeping, and weight shifting. Your friends are sure to want to "swipe" this move!

Step 1

Sit in a squat position with your right foot tucked underneath you. Extend your left leg straight out in front of you. Place your hands on the ground by your hips. Keep your weight on your right toes.

Step 2

Bring your left foot back so that it's tucked underneath you next to your right foot. Keep your hands on the ground.

Step 3

Extend your right leg forward.

Step 4

Sweep your right leg to the left, crossing your right ankle over your left ankle. At the same time, lift your left hand, and place it on the floor next to your right hand. You should land with your right foot crossed in front of your left foot and your torso facing to the right.

Step 5

Continue sweeping your right leg. Hop up with your left foot to let your right leg pass underneath it. As you hop, twist your body to the right.

Step 6   *not shown*

You should land facing the opposite direction as in Step 1, with your right foot tucked underneath you. Your left leg is extended straight out in front of you. Repeat the Baby Swipe so that you land facing front again.

Tip

Once you become comfortable with all the steps, practice Steps 4 and 5 as one fluid movement. This motion will make it look as though you are almost flipping in the air.

BackSpin

DIFFICULTY: ★★☆

The **Backspin** is a famous and fun breaking move. It requires **momentum** to perform rotations on your back as fast as possible. The goal is to look like a spinning top. Be sure to practice the Backspin on a smooth surface.

Step 1

Sit on the floor in a straddle position. To wind up, lean over to the right. Place your hands on the floor by your right hip.

Step 2

Switch sides by leaning over to the left and placing your hands on the floor. Bend in your left leg slightly at the knee.

momentum—*the force or speed created by movement*

Step 3

Sweep your right leg over your left leg. As your right leg passes over your left leg, drop onto your left shoulder and left hip. Extend your left arm out to the side and place your hand on the floor. Use your hand to pull your body to the left. The harder and faster you sweep your right leg over your left, the faster you'll spin.

Step 4

When your right leg points up at the ceiling, flatten your back on the floor. Remove your left hand from the floor. Extend both arms straight out to the sides. Lift your left leg so both legs open in a "V" shape.

Step 5

As you spin to the left, slowly lower your arms and legs into your body.

As your spin slows down, think about landing in a specific pose. You can land flat on your back with one leg crossed over the other. You could even lie on the ground with both arms and legs stretched out. Whatever pose you choose, hit it with purpose.

Chapter 4

FREEZES

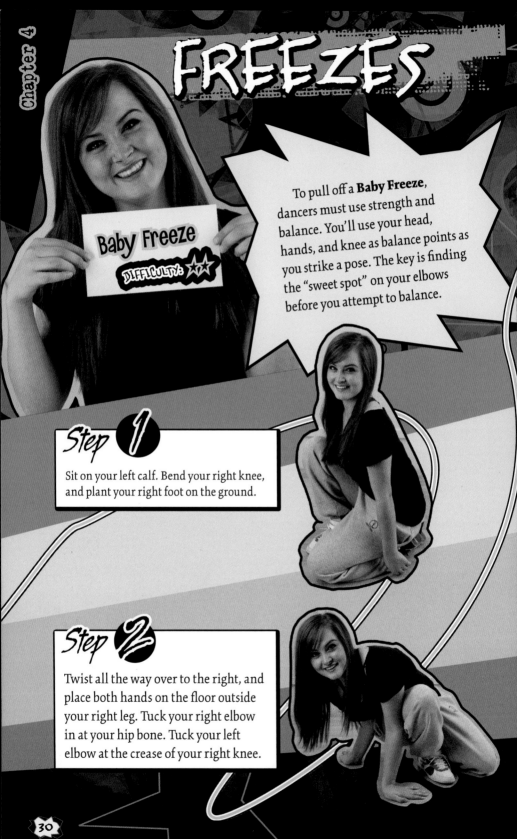

Baby Freeze

DIFFICULTY: ★☆

To pull off a **Baby Freeze**, dancers must use strength and balance. You'll use your head, hands, and knee as balance points as you strike a pose. The key is finding the "sweet spot" on your elbows before you attempt to balance.

Step 1

Sit on your left calf. Bend your right knee, and plant your right foot on the ground.

Step 2

Twist all the way over to the right, and place both hands on the floor outside your right leg. Tuck your right elbow in at your hip bone. Tuck your left elbow at the crease of your right knee.

Step 3

Lean all the way over to the right, lifting your feet off of the floor. Use the top of your head as a third balancing point. If you have trouble balancing, adjust your elbows until you can balance on them.

Step 4

Keeping your right knee and hip in place on your elbows, extend your right foot forward. Bend your left knee back to hit the classic Baby Freeze position.

Tip

Don't let too much weight fall onto your head. If you do, you are likely to end up balancing on your cheek. B-boys and b-girls call this position a "face plant." It's considered bad technique and should be avoided for your safety.

Chair Freeze

DIFFICULTY: ⭐☆

The **Chair Freeze** is more difficult to get into than it is to hold. It involves balancing on one leg, one arm, and the top of your head. First practice twisting your body and balancing correctly. Then you will be able to slip into and out of the Chair Freeze with ease.

Step 1

Sit on your right calf. Bend your left knee and plant your left foot on the ground. Stab your right elbow into your side. Your wrist should be flexed so that your fingers are pointing toward the ground.

Step 2

Lean over to the right, and place your right hand on the ground. Your elbow should still be stabbed into your side.

Practice the Chair Freeze very slowly at first. Start by getting comfortable with stabbing your elbow into your side and placing your hand on the floor. Also, be sure to warm up your wrists before attempting this move.

Step 3

Prop up your right leg so that both feet are flat on the floor and your backside is lifted. Finally, let the top of your head touch the floor.

Step 4

Rest your right heel on your left knee. Place your left hand on your right hip.

Stop!

Safety First

The freezes and power moves coming next are for advanced breakers only. Master the basic and intermediate moves before attempting the L-Kick, Hollowback, Windmill, or Head Spin. And when you do try these moves, make sure you use caution. Use a mat or a padded surface to try tough freezes. Have an adult assist you during tricky handstands and balances, or use a wall to practice. Wear a helmet or skullcap to protect your head while learning the Head Spin.

L-Kick

DIFFICULTY: ★★★

This flashy freeze is called the **L-Kick** because your legs make an "L" shape. It's a one-handed handstand performed with one leg kicked out. You can point the other leg to the ceiling or bend your knee.

Step 1

Stand in a relaxed position. Raise your right arm. Get ready to head to the floor as if you are starting a cartwheel.

Tip

It's always helpful to stretch before attempting the L-Kick. To stretch the muscles in your sides, stand with your legs apart. Lean your upper body to the right and to the left. Then bend forward and hold your ankles to stretch your hamstrings.

Step 2 *not shown*

Put your right hand on the floor. Swing up your left leg first, and then your right leg. Your head should face forward instead of looking down at the ground.

Step 3

As your left leg swings up, start to bend at the waist. Keep your legs slightly open in an "L" shape. Extend your left leg to the left side of your body, and bend your right knee. Touch your left foot with your left hand.

Step 4 *not shown*

Freeze in this position for a few seconds before you come back to a standing position. Land on your right foot before your left foot.

HoLLowback

DIFFICULTY: ⭐⭐⭐

The **Hollowback** is a difficult handstand freeze. Breakers lean backward in an extreme arch, extending one or both legs behind them. It's easier to learn this move with one leg extended because it puts less strain on your shoulders and arms.

BEFORE YOU BEGIN:

Make sure you can pull off a solid handstand. First balance against a wall. Then try a handstand away from the wall.

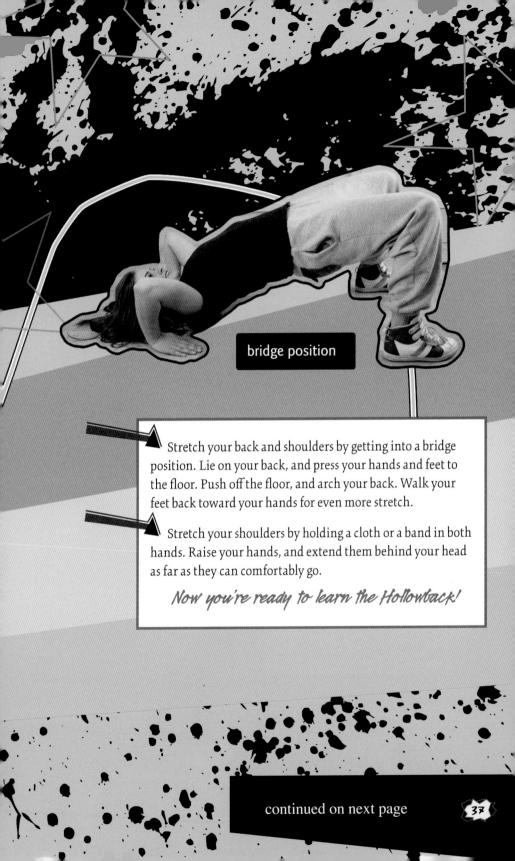

bridge position

Stretch your back and shoulders by getting into a bridge position. Lie on your back, and press your hands and feet to the floor. Push off the floor, and arch your back. Walk your feet back toward your hands for even more stretch.

Stretch your shoulders by holding a cloth or a band in both hands. Raise your hands, and extend them behind your head as far as they can comfortably go.

Now you're ready to learn the Hollowback!

continued on next page

Step ①

Start in a handstand against a wall. Tuck one knee into your stomach. Point the other leg to the ceiling. You should be facing away from the wall when you are upside down.

Step ②

Start to walk on your hands away from the wall. Touch the wall with your straight leg for balance.

Step 3

Slowly arch your back, letting your straight leg move farther down the wall. To bring your straight leg all the way behind you, arch your chest forward as far as you can.

Step 4 *not shown*

Walk back toward the wall, and come out of your handstand.

Tip

Practice the Hollowback while touching the wall until you feel comfortable. Then let go of the wall for a second to find your balance. Stay near the wall to catch yourself in case you fall. Once you can balance for more than five seconds, practice the Hollowback away from the wall.

Chapter 5

POWER MOVES

Windmill

DIFFICULTY: ★★★★☆

Anyone who's ever watched a breaker get down has seen a **Windmill**. Breakers spin on their backs and shoulders while whipping their legs around in a "V" shape. You're sure to impress a crowd with this amazing breaking move.

Step 1

Stab your right elbow into your waist near your belly button.

Step 2

Place your right hand on the floor with fingers facing to the right. Your legs should be open and straight out behind you, with your toes lightly touching the floor. All of your weight is on your right arm. Place your left hand on the floor for support.

Step 3

To start your clockwise spin, push off with your left hand. Keep your right hand planted on the ground as you spin to the right.

continued on next page

Lift the left hip and leg up so the right leg can pass underneath.

Step 4

After you make about a quarter turn, lift your left hip. Kick your left leg out to the side, and let your right leg cross underneath it. Your right leg should now be crossed over to the left side of your body. This twisting move helps you gain momentum going into the spin.

Step 5

As you lift your left hip, drop onto your right shoulder. Roll across your shoulders from right to left. Your legs should be whipping around in a "V" shape.

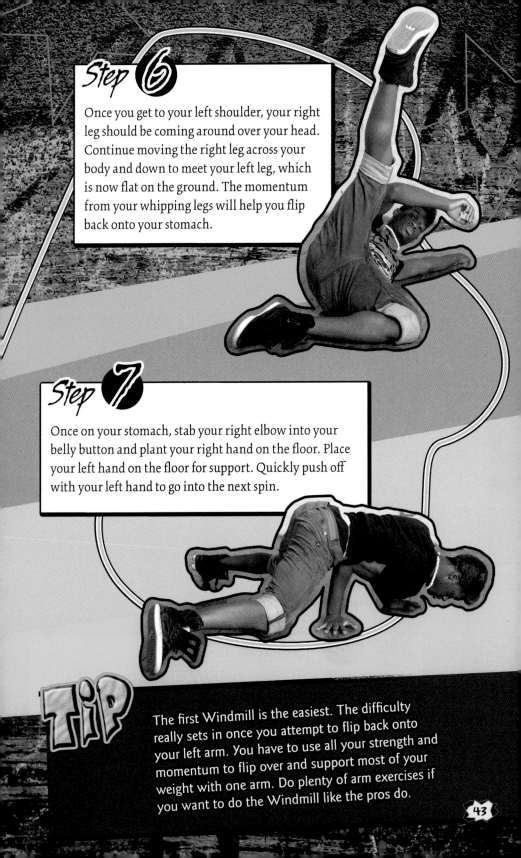

Step 6

Once you get to your left shoulder, your right leg should be coming around over your head. Continue moving the right leg across your body and down to meet your left leg, which is now flat on the ground. The momentum from your whipping legs will help you flip back onto your stomach.

Step 7

Once on your stomach, stab your right elbow into your belly button and plant your right hand on the floor. Place your left hand on the floor for support. Quickly push off with your left hand to go into the next spin.

Tip

The first Windmill is the easiest. The difficulty really sets in once you attempt to flip back onto your left arm. You have to use all your strength and momentum to flip over and support most of your weight with one arm. Do plenty of arm exercises if you want to do the Windmill like the pros do.

Head Spin

DIFFICULTY: ★★★★☆

Head spins are the ultimate goal of breaking. This daring power move has you spinning while balancing on top of your head. But before you jump in, practice Head Spins in stages. First, work on your balance. Then practice spinning on your head. Be sure to practice the Head Spin on a smooth surface. Use a helmet or skullcap to protect your head.

Step 1

Balance on your head while resting your hands on the ground. As you become more comfortable on your head, try moving your legs around. Open them in a "V" shape, close them, and kick them to the front and back. Wind up your legs by twisting your torso back and forth. Keep your head and hands in the same place.

Step 2 *not shown*

When you feel secure in your twists, wind up your legs once and release them. At the same time, lift your hands, and bring your legs together. You will most likely make less than one rotation before you fall. But don't worry. The more you practice, the longer you'll be able to spin.

Step 3

Once you master a quick spin on your head, use your hands to rotate your body around. Keep your legs open in a "V" shape, and lift your hands for a second. When you place your hands back on the floor, use them to turn your body. At first, you will need to use many of these touches, which are called taps.

Step 4 *not shown*

As you get more comfortable, you'll just use taps to rev up for a spin. Use one tap for each full rotation. Do this a few times until you gain speed. Then let go, and spin away! You can keep your legs in a "V" shape, bring them together, or move them however you please.

THE ART OF BREAKING

To really master the art of breaking, you'll need to do more than just pull off a few moves. You'll need confidence, attitude, and skill. With practice and passion, you can become a true b-boy or b-girl.

battle (BAT-uhl)—a competition between individual dancers or groups; the dancers who receive the loudest crowd applause win

burn (BURN)—to mimic or make fun of another dancer during an uprock move

capoeira (kah-puh-WAY-ruh)—a Brazilian dance of African origin that uses martial arts moves such as kicks and chops

cypher (SY-fuhr)—a circle that forms around a breaker to give space to dance during a battle

hamstring (HAM-string)—a muscle in the back of the thigh that helps to flex and extend the leg

momentum (moh-MEN-tuhm)—the force or speed created by movement

rhythm (RITH-uhm)—a regular beat in music or dance

straddle (STRAD-uhl)—a position in which a dancer is seated on the floor with his or her legs stretched out in a "V" shape

tap (TAP)—a quick touch using the hands to keep balance and gain speed during a head spin

transition (tran-ZI-shuhn)—a step performed in order to move from one dance step to another

variation (vair-ee-AY-shuhn)—something that is slightly different from another thing of the same type

Cornish, Melanie J. *The History of Hip Hop.* Crabtree Contact. New York: Crabtree Pub., 2009.

Fitzgerald, Tamsin. *Hip-Hop and Urban Dance.* Dance. Chicago: Heinemann Library, 2009.

Freese, Joan. *Hip-Hop Dancing.* Dance. Mankato, Minn.: Capstone Press, 2008.

Garofoli, Wendy. *Hip-Hop Dancing Volume 3: Popping, Locking, and Everything in Between.* Hip-Hop Dancing. Mankato, Minn.: Capstone Press, 2011.

INTERNET SITES

FactHound offers a safe, fun way to find Internet sites related to this book. All of the sites on FactHound have been researched by our staff.

Here's all you do:

Visit *www.facthound.com*

Type in this code: 9781429654852